LLEWELLYN'S VAN

The Truth About

THE DRUIDS

by Tadhg MacCrossan

Author of

The Sacred Cauldron

Llewellyn Publications is the oldest publisher of New Age Sciences in the Western Hemisphere. This book is one of a series of introductory explorations of each of the many fascinating dimensions of New Age Science—each important to a new understanding of Body and Soul, Mind and Spirit, of Nature and humanity's place in the world, and the vast unexplored regions of the Microcosm and Macrocosm.

Please write for a full list of publications.

1993
Llewellyn Publications
P.O. Box 64383-577, St. Paul, MN 55164-0383
U.S.A.

Dó Mo Ghrá, Valerie

FIRST EDITION
First Printing, 1993

International Standard Book Number: 0-87542-577-1

LLEWELLYN PUBLICATIONS
A Division of Llewellyn Worldwide, Ltd.
P.O. Box 64383, St. Paul, MN 55164-0383

WHO WERE THE DRUIDS?

To mention the word *Druid* is to evoke images of ancient wizards and wonder-workers from old Irish sagas or Welsh legends, from Caesar's *Gallic Wars* or Scottish folktales. If you have read about them, you probably have formed one of the many images of them from literature and legends. Who were they? What did they teach? What did they do?

The popular characterization of the Druids is more often a fiction than an accurate representation of factual history. They have been romanticized in such anachronistic roles as engineers of Stonehenge and other megaliths, as the priesthood of the "Lost Tribes" of ancient Israel, as shamans of pre-Celtic Western Europe, and as Witches of pre-Indo-European Britain. But the Druids were none of these things.

Druids have been credited with many teachings such as Pythagorean philosophy, Cabala, mysteries of the Goddess, Buddhism, Deism (*Barddas* forgeries), Pantheism, Runes, and Wicca. But all of these were foreign to the Druids, and formed none of the teachings of real Druidism. We now know that many of those things we were told in modern folklore were not true about the Druids, and so the question is still unanswered: who were the Druids?

Come with me and let's travel back to an ancient time in an ancient land. Let's go to old Ireland in the days before Patrick came to spread the religion of the Latin language.

❦

We arrive at Tara on the eve of Samhain. The people speak *Goidelic*, and in their language they call their festival *Samonios*.

Two bonfires are blazing on a hilltop. In between the fires is an open area covered by a huge wooden roof, like a pavilion of thatching supported by wooden poles. Everyone from the village and surrounding farms are gathered. We see musicians playing rectangular lyres which they call *crottas*; singers chanting songs which remind us of the airs and dirges of the Scottish bagpipes. The bards are dressed in colorful tunics and brightly speckled cloaks of tartan and stripes trimmed in fur or feathers. There are beautiful women sitting at a wooden table. Some are blondes with flaxen hair, some are redheads, and there are brunettes among them. They are clad in beautiful gold and silver jewelry according to their rank and wealth. We find a table of warriors with swords of shining polished iron hanging in their scabbards, and men standing holding tall spears.

In the middle of this area there is a tall wooden pole on which many images are carved in swirling knotwork. We watch a man dressed in a white knee-length tunic and a cloak of white and grey bullhide sitting at a prominent place calling out to men next to the pole. Next to him is a man dressed in the most colorful cloak with a golden collar, wearing a magnificent gilded helmet with wings and crest and a drooping auburn moustache.

The men at the pole are dressed in white knee-length tunics and tartan cloaks, and are pouring out liquid from a large, beautifully wrought bronze and silver bowl. We are privileged to see an ancient Druidic ritual in progress!

Luckily, we have an interpreter with us who explains that the man in the winged helmet is the king or chieftain of that region, the men pouring and burying are priests, and that the man sitting next to the king is the chief's high priest.

When we ask the interpreter what they are called in his native language, he says that the king is called the *rix* (reekhs), the man sitting next to him who is the master of ceremonies and king's high priest is called the *druis* (droo-iss), and the other men comprise *uates* (wah-tiss) or *uelites* (wel-ee-tess); the bard singing the ancient Celtic hymn is the *gutuatir* (goo-too-ah-tur).

✿✿✿

Our interpreter is gone; we are back from our time-travels now. We caught a glimpse of the ancient Celtic world. We saw an ancient Druid and his team of priests. All the men we saw were members of the class known collectively as the *Druids*. There were other kinds of members of the Druidic class we did not see in this brief episode. But luckily, we do not have to travel back in time to learn about their religion and magic. We can pierce through the veil of time by studying the traditions as they have come down to us in the written form. One of the first books to do this is *The Sacred Cauldron*.

The Oral Tradition and the Druidic Class

The ancient Druids considered it profane to record their teachings in writing. All of their teachings were handed down by the spoken word in verses or stories. Different kinds of "druids" taught different categories of the ancient lore. The highest in rank of the learned men of the Celtic peoples was called the *Druis*, or "Druid."

He was the advisor to his chieftain or king. He had to know the rituals, laws, customs, and myths. He had to be skilled in the verses and songs of his people, as well. The mythology of the Celtic peoples was preserved by people like him.

2

There were also women "druids" who specialized in the cult of the local Goddess of their people. This female druid was called the *ueleda* (we-leh-dah) and *bendruí* (byen-dree) in Old Irish. The ueleda or bendrui was sometimes a priestess of such goddesses as Sulis, Brigindu, or Brigantia and lived apart from the tribe with other priestesses guarding the sacred round hearth fire of this Goddess.

Certain other learned men were called "seers" or "prophets" in the ancient Celtic language. These were *uelis* (weh-liss), a seer and poet-magician (plural *uelites*); and *uatis* (wah-tiss), a prophet and poet-magician (plural *uates*).

The term *Velis* could almost be used synonymously with the term *Druid* in the general sense. Indeed, after Christianity came to Ireland, the term *Velis* evolved into Old Irish *Fili* (fee-lyih) and replaced the term *Druid* for a sort of secularized version of a Druid, while the term *Vatis* or *uatis* evolved into Old Irish *Faith*, "prophet."

Today the Modern Irish word *file* means "poet" and is often translated "bard," though he was of higher rank than a bard. It is important to understand the differences in these technical terms from the old Celtic languages, because these terms are used in the old writings which preserve the oral traditions of this Celtic priesthood.

Ironically, it is because the Irish were converted to the Christian religion that we have authentic traditions of the Druids recorded in writing. The new religion brought the Latin alphabet to Ireland, because the early Church used Latin as its official language. Ireland was the only Celtic country to convert from Druidism to Christianity. The other Celtic countries of Britain (when it was inhabited by the Welsh and Cornish before the English came), and Gaul had been dominated by the Romans who eliminated Druidism and replaced it with many Roman customs and cults in the first century. But Ireland remained a land governed by many petty kingdoms, or *toutas* (tribes), which were Celtic. Even later, when the first Norse, Saxons, and Normans invaded Ireland, many of them became Celticized to the Gaelic language and customs, sometimes forgetting their Germanic heritage. Ireland, then, remained culturally Celtic and the Church had to adapt to the Celtic way.

Many of the Christian clerics of early Ireland had been *filídh* or "poets" in the native Celtic tradition before converting and becoming monks, priests, bishops, etc. St. Columcille was a Fili before becoming a Christian. Many of these men loved the Druidic traditions so much that they used the Latin alphabet in their spare time to write down the Old Irish that was their native tongue, and to write down their knowledge. The older religion of Druidism was often practiced side by side with Christianity, and scholars have

3

noticed that while they sometimes attempted to disguise the lore they also preserved very ancient Indo-European themes, customs, and philosophies.

Many of these ancient and mediaeval Irish writings have still not been translated in English and are only available in Old and Middle Irish. It is from this literature that scholars in Indo-European comparative mythology and philology have been able to learn a great deal about the culture of the Celtic peoples.

CELTIC ORIGINS

The Celtic peoples were the peoples of Gaul (France, Switzerland, Belgium, Bohemia, and Galicia in Spain), Britain (now Wales, Cornwall, and Brittany in France), Scotland, and Ireland. A group of Gaulish settlers colonized Galatia in what is now Turkey.

The Celts were closely related to the Germanic peoples, the Balts, Slavs, Romans, Oscans, Thracians, Greeks, and distantly related to the Aryans of Iran and India. All of these peoples were descendents of tribes who lived in Russia and the Ukraine nearly 5000 years ago. The evidence from archaeology and linguistics demonstrates that these people had their own religion of which their traditions were preserved orally down through the centuries. Celtic magic as transmitted down from the Druids to the Old Irish literature preserves much of these archaic traditions.

CELTIC RELIGION

Druidism is used synonymously with the phrases "Celtic religion" and "Celtic magic." In order to enter into the magico-religious system, one needs to be familiar with the Gods and Goddesses of that system's mythology. The mythology of the Celts is found best represented in the *Irish Book of Invasions* or *Lebor Gábala Érenn*. These tales give a pseudo-history of Ireland from the creation to the arrival of the Gods and finally of humankind.

The high Gods of the pagan Irish were called the *Tuatha Dé Danann*, "toutas of the Goddess Danu." These were the Gods of both the sky and heavens. Allied to them were the Gods of the earth, fire, and horses, and a family of Gods of the sea. The enemies of the Tuatha Dé Danann were the Giants called the *Fomors*, who opposed the Gods and the values they represented. The Tuatha Dé Danann (or Gods) represented order, learning, wisdom, skill, technology, industry, strength, courage, productivity, and fertility as well as light, warmth, progress, and beauty. The Giants represented stinginess, oppression, rudeness, cowardice, ignorance, vulgarity, poverty, crudity, as well as darkness, stagnation, ugliness, brutality, sickness, and disorder. The values of the Gods were the values of Celtic society and represented the healthy ideals of society and the individual.

The head of the Celtic pantheon was Lugus the Long Armed followed by Noudons the Silver Armed, then the deities of Uindosenos "Cernunnos," Ogmios, Brigindu, Maponos, and Epona. Celtic religion idealized its virtues in a basic three-fold scheme of learning, strength and wealth which made a sort of five-fold division of the Gods like other Indo-European mythologies:

1. **Lugus** (Loo-goos)   The Magician-King

   Noudons (Nuh-oo-dohnts)   The Judge-Priest

2. **Ogmios** (Ohg-mee-awss)   The Warrior

3. **Epos Olloatir** (Ollo-ah-tur)   The Horse God

   Epona (Eh-paw-nah)   The Horse Goddess

An understanding of the Celtic pantheon can come from a careful reading of early Irish literature, which includes not only the *Lebor Gabála Érenn* but also tales from the Fenian cycle and Ulster cycle. The Ulster cycle includes the tales of CúChullain, the great Celtic hero and an incarnation of Lugus; Conchobhar Mac Nessa; Aillil and Medhbh ("Maeve"); and the epic *Táin Bó Cuailnge* ("Cattle Raid of Cooley"). The Fenian cycle are stories about the "Fenians" or *Fianna*, the warrior-bands of Old Ireland, centering around the famous Finn of Finn mac Cumhail. Finn mac Cumhail's men included Cailte mac Ronan, famous for his later philosophical debates with St. Patrick; Conan Mael, famed for his acid-tongued wit; Diarmuid ("Dermott"), for his handsomeness; and so forth. Finn is the most famous of the incarnations of the Celtic God Uindos, or "Cernunnos," as he has been most popularized.

The exploits of CúChullain tells us of his mystical metagenetic incarnation of the Pan-Celtic High God Lugh (Lugus). Lugh appears in the *Táin* and other tales of the Ulster cycle, like Odin in the Volsunga Saga, or Hermes in Greek tales.

This tells us something about the attributes and character of the head deities of the Celtic and Germanic pantheon and why the Romans identified Lugus and Wodan both with Mercury (Hermes). Lugh and Odin have much in common, both in attributes and appearance, suggesting a common ancestry in the ancient past.

Finn mac Cumhail is an incarnation of the wild hunter and warrior-poet God Cernunnos, and as such we find this deity manifested in other Irish and Welsh mediaeval tales. The Fenians are so skilled in the magical arts of poetry and fighting that they seem to be a combination of warriors and Druids, with the freedom to move from one tribal territory to another like normal Druids. Scholars have identified the tales of the Fenians with other Indo-European *männerbunds* like the *Eriloz* or Erulians of the Germanic peoples. Both the Fenian and Ulster cycles of tales and sagas are full of magic and enchantment and are a great source for learning about the nature of the Tuatha Dé Danann divinities. They broadly resemble the Aesir and Vanir of the Germanic peoples, the Devas of the Vedic Indians, and the Olympians of the Greeks.

Much has been made of the Celtic Goddesses, particularly the tribal Goddesses of the land and rivers. Many neopagans have attempted to synchretize all of them into just one single Goddess they call "Mother Earth," but the Celtic tradition knows of no one single "Mother Earth," nor is there any evidence that they conceived of the earth as a deity. Instead, the Celts' most important Goddess was not a Moon Goddess, nor an Earth Goddess, but a Goddess representing the land of the touta. She was the Goddess of Sovereignty. Kings and chieftains had to be ritually married to her in order to become rulers. She was believed to be incarnate as a white mare. The mare was then sacrificed in order to release its spirit, and the flesh consumed by the king and people in order to take in some of her divine essence. This mare Goddess was the "Great Mother," who is the archetype of the feminine most sought by every man in his wife, and the object of love in the inspiration of the poets. She is the representative of that which is sexually appealing to men, and she became the horseman's guide when incarnated as mare. She had many *hypostases* (or manifestations) as different local Goddesses among different toutas. Each touta had its local hypostasis of this Goddess. She was later called the *banshee* (bean-sidhe), which means "woman of peace" (*peace* was used euphemistically for spirits and spooks in later Irish and Scots-Gaelic folklore).

This local Goddess was not a Maiden, Matron and Crone of the moon (as a 20th century theory would have it), and she wasn't necessarily a remnant of a "matriarchal" religion, for this Goddess was the ideal of men's desire. These Goddesses were Indo-European style Goddesses, and they were triple Goddesses because they represented the three Indo-European virtues:

6

1. Wisdom or poetry and learning (kings and druids)

2. Physical strength or health and courage (warriors)

3. Productivity, fertility and sexuality (producers)

The Goddesses who represented these things among the Tuatha Dé Danann were the Morrígu and Brigit. Brigit herself was a daughter of the *Dagda* (doyda), who was named *Eochu Ollathir*, "horse all-father." Morrígu was one of the Dagda's mates, as well as one for Nemed and Nuada. When Nuada was replaced by Lugh, Lugh became the king and Morrígu's husband. Morrígu is the tribal goddess of the Tuatha Dé Danann, just as each tuath had its own local Goddess: Sinand of the Shannon, Matrona of the Marne, Aine of Cnoc Aine (Knockany), Teamuir of Tara, Tailltiu of Teltown, Macha of Ard-Macha (Armagh), Sequana of the Seine, and Brigantia of Brigantes. It is important to note that when the Morrígu of the Tuatha Dé Danann takes her warrior form, she appears as a crow on the battlefields picking up the spirits of slain warriors and taking them to the heavenly realm beyond this world, such as Tír na nóg or Tír na mBeo. In this respect she is very similar to such Goddesses as the Valkyries of the Teutonic peoples, and Erinyes or Eumenides of the Greeks.

It is also attested in Gaulish traditions (as told through Greeks) and found in archaeology that the God Lugus was accompanied by ravens or crows, just like the Germanic Odin with his two ravens (Huginn and Munnin) and his Valkyries. Two divine characters in the Welsh *Mabinogi* (Mah-bin-oh-ggee) have names meaning raven and white-breast; *Bran* and *Branwen*. Bran appears in Irish tales as a sea God, and there are connections with the sea in the Welsh tales, as well. Lugus, like Odin, was the king of the Gods in the Celtic pantheon, he was accompanied by crows and ravens, he carried a spear, he closed one eye to do his magic (Odin offered his eye); and also like Zeus in Hesiod's *Theogony*, he led the Tuatha Dé Danann Gods in victory over the Fomorian Giants. The birth and childhood of Lugh also parallels that of the Greek Zeus.

Lugh was hidden from his evil maternal grandfather, Balor the Fomor, by his paternal uncle Goibhniu (called *Gwydion* in Welsh), the smith God who brought him to his foster parents and taught him all the crafts and skills. Goibhniu made Lugh a magical spear, with which he was destined to slay his evil Fomorian maternal grandfather. Zeus had been hidden from his father Kronos on the isle of Crete and given magical weapons by the Cyclopes. Like Lugh slaying Balor, Zeus slew Kronos and freed his brothers and sisters of the Olympic pantheon and started a War between the Gods (Olympians) and the Giants (Titans).

Nuada was called *Noudons* in Old Celtic, and *Nudd* or *Lludd Llaw Ereint* in Middle Welsh. His name meant "fisher" or "hunter." He was the maimed king of the Celtic pantheon, and was replaced by his cousin Lugh. The story of the First and Second Battle of Magh Tuired (Moytura) in the *Book of Invasions* is the central myth of the two head gods. Welsh literature has its mediaevalized or romanticized version in the tale of *Lludd and Lleuellys*.

Nuada or Nudd very much resembles the Germanic Tyr; both are one-armed Gods who become shadowy partners to the main high God (Lugh or Odin). There are parallels in the Rig Veda of India in the symbiosis of Mitra and Varuna, or in the very ancient Roman religion with Jupiter and Dius Fidius. Noudons was the father of Uindos (Finn, Gwynn), and is the king who becomes the maimed fisherman and mystic. His character has survived into Arthurian legend as the fisher king, and like Arthur, he sends his men on the quest for the Grail.

The Fenian cycle is very similar to the Arthurian cycle, but it is more purely Celtic, and it is devoid of Christian influence. The story called the *Acallamh na Senorach*, or "Conversation of the Old Men," is a dialogue between Cailte mac Ronan and Patrick arguing over Druidism (pagan Celtic religion) and Christianity. This is a part of the Fenian cycle that is full of humor as well as philosophical discourse. Another Fenian story late in the tradition is called *Oisín in Tír na nÓg* and is about Finn mac Cumhail's son *Oisín* (Usheen), "little deer," who was invited and brought to the Otherworld. Upon his return to the middle world, he suddenly became an old man when he set foot on the ground. In these wonder tales, time is distorted by a trip to the Otherworld (whether beyond the western wave or in the underworld). An hour in the Otherworld can be years in this world, or what seems like hours or days there may only be a few minutes here.

A fair amount of information has been gleaned from ancient Gaulish inscriptions, the cult objects that were long ago buried with the dead or thrown down wells and springs as offerings to deities. Some objects were deliberately smashed and buried as offerings to the *Deuoi* (Gods). The usual place for theurgic ritual, worship of the Deuoi, or veneration of the ancestors was in the sacred ground called the *nemeton*, which was a clearing in the midst of a grove or glade in a wood, or on hilltops or near a body of water or in the center of a toutal territory. Often there would be a well for dropping things down to the underworld, or things would be buried in the border. There were also sacred fires on which things were offered by burning them, like in the Hindu and Parsi religions.

Over 300 divine names have been found in the old Gaulish inscriptions, but many of these names are actually epithets and nick-names, as well as mere names of local ghosts and other spirits. From the testimony of Roman and Greek commentaries, there is much material covering the culture and religion of the Gauls and Britons (ancient Welsh), but the most accurate and reliable sources are those from Caesar, Pomponius Mela, Athenaeus, Strabo, and Diodorus Siculus. Pliny the Elder commented on a few trivial matters and exaggerated the negative aspects of the old Gaulish Druids, while many of the later Greco-Roman writers made up stories or misinter-preted rumors about the Druids. Some of these misinterpretations concerned the doctrine of transmigration of souls, which was thought to have been like the doctrine taught by the Greek philoso-pher Pythagoras; the Druids apparently taught a philosophy which, though similar (in holding the abstract world of music, time, and ratios as divine), differed in other ways to the one taught by the Pythagoreans. One remarkable observation made by an ancient Greek compared the Druids to the Magi of Persia and the Brahmans of India. In general terms, there were many similarities, but this is because the Druids were a priest-craft which shared the same func-tions in Celtic society as the Magi and Brahmans in their cultures. All three had inherited many of the same archaic Indo-European ideas from their ancestors. Celtic religion — with its system of Druids, polytheism, rituals, and belief in incarnations of Gods as famous heroes — is very similar to the religion of the Indians before the time of the rise of Buddhism, the Krishna and Shiva cults, Jainism, and other reform movements. The rituals of Druidism were similar to the rituals of the Zoroastrian religion of the Magi (the Mobads). Today, the Zoroastrian religion survives among Indians of Persian descent, called *Parsis,* who preserved it against Islamic oppression. The Mobads of the Parsis and Brahmans of Orthodox Hinduism are the distant cousins of the Druids of the Celts, but unlike the Druids they survive, unbroken by mass conversion, to this day.

REBIRTH

In Old Celtic (Gaulish-Brittonic and Goidelic), the word for rebirth was *ategenos* (Old Irish *aithghen*). This doctrine was a type of limited reincarnation in which the spirit of an ancestor was born among his or her own kin. This means that certain inherited characteristics and even Deuoi (Tuatha Dé Danann Gods) would sometimes appear or reappear in a family lineage. Even more often it meant that a particular deity would choose to befriend a particular lineage and incarnate himself (or herself) within that lineage, and thus a child would be born possessing certain characteristics of that deity. This child would not necessarily (though this sometimes happened in the case of great heroes) embody the personality of that spirit or divinity, but certain attributes or talents would develop as a gift from that divinity. Such a phenomena was interpreted as rebirth in much the same way a mother might say that her infant son "has his father's eyes," or a father might say that his son "has his grandfather's talent for music." Today most people are likely to interpret these familiar family traits as genetically inherited, but this was considered a form of rebirth as taught by the Druids and well-known in the Celtic faith. Spiritual possession was another aspect of this belief, but ategenos differed very greatly from the modern-day conceptions of reincarnation and karma borrowed from theosophy and certain sects of Hinduism, which state that people are punished for sins by paying for them in the next incarnation. The Druids never taught that people were rewarded and punished according to principles associated with the reincarnation process of karma. The Druids would have thought such ideas absurd.

The *Deuoi,* or higher divinities, were creative, shape-shifting spirits and could become incarnate in many forms through their magic. In fact, the Deuoi were manifestations of a force greater than themselves. They are capable of taking many forms or guises and could walk the earthly realm of the manifested world, and this is very probably the reason that the Druids avoided representations of the Deuoi as human in art until the Romans conquered them. It is also why the Romans equated Lugus, like Woden, with their own Mercury (Hermes), who was considered the messenger of the Gods. Celtic gods were like the Devas of Vedic religion.

THE REALMS

According to ancient Celtic beliefs, three main realms co-exist: an underworld associated with the past, an earthly realm of the middle world associated with manifested reality, and an upperworld associated with the potential reality and all possible futures where the abstract concepts and the divine dwell. This is a vertical view of time and space. Thinking in a more horizontal view, the plains of the realms are divided into quarters with a vertical axis that interconnects and links all realms together. This axis is the concept of a world-tree, or *Bilios,* similar to the Germanic concept of Yggdrasil or the Greek conception of an Omphalos. The center is where all realms converge. Time flows like the waters of a river from the upper to the lower, and from east toward west. The southern realms are associated with the heat, energy and warmth of the summer half of the year, while the northern realms are associated with the static and cold of the winter half of the year. The south and east are of the Deuoi, or Tuatha Dé Danann, while the north and west are realms of the Fomors. This is why the myths depicted the Gods arriving in Ireland on the southeast coast, and the giants dwelling on Tory Island at the northwest coast. The divinities of Lír (Ocean), the benevolent sea Gods, dwelt in the southwest beyond the waves. The Tuatha Dé Danann were also associated with four realms known as *Falias* (fail), "understone;" *Gorias* (gor), "warmth;" *Findias* (find), "white;" and *Muirias* (muir), "sea;" which denote divisions of their realm. *Lia Fáil* (Lee-uh Foyl or Lee-uh Faw-yil) means "the rock of the understone;" it is a divine analogue of the stone of truth — a flat rock with footprints carved into it which is stood upon when swearing oaths or delivering testimony. This must stand for the manifested realm. Findias and Gorias may stand for the realms of atmosphere and fire or light of the sky. Muirias is certainly the sea or ocean which surrounds the earth in the manifested world. The sea and other bodies of water were considered openings to the underworld, a watery abode under the earth.

The three main realms:

Upperworld, called *Nemos* or *Uindomagos*
(Welsh *nef, gwynfa;* Irish *neamh, Magh Find/ Magh Findargat*)

Middleworld, called *Mediomagos*
(Irish *Magh Mide*)

Lowerworld, called *Andumnos* or *Antumnos*
(Welsh *Annwn, Annwfn;* Irish *Andomhain*)

Even the geography of the countryside reflected the Celtic conceptions of the magic of time and space. Ireland was divided into fifths, called *coícit* in Old Irish, now translated to mean "province." Four of these fifths are still represented on maps of Ireland today:

Leinster or Laigin in the east

Munster or Mumu in the south

Connaught or Connacht in the west

Ulster or Ulaid in the north

Mide, "middle," was the central fifth now remembered in County Meath and West Meath, which are now Leinster. The province of Mide or Meath was the ritual center where the tuathas or toutas of Ireland gathered annually and held festivals.

TIME

The oldest Indo-European root concept for the measure of time was the moon, and this reveals the nature of the Celtic calendar. The Celts never deviated from the basic idea of this lunar time measurement, and the Druids preserved it from their Indo-European tradition. Luckily for Celtophiles today, ancient Celtic calendars were unearthed in France. The most outstanding one is called the Coligny calendar; the others are fragments of duplicate calendars.

The so-called "tree-calendar" in which ogam tree names are used as names of months in certain forms of neopagan Witchcraft are not ancient in origin, and unfortunately have no connections with the Druids. They are the creation of Robert Graves in his book *The White Goddess*. There are many neopagan Dianic groups which use this invention of Graves, but the real ancient Celtic calendar (a product of the Druids) was different and a bit more complicated to calculate. Many month names on the modern Celtic calendars are pre-Christian in origin, such as *Mí na Shamna*, "the month of Samhain," cognate with the Gaulish *Samonios* (which appears on the Coligny calendar). The festival of Samhain was the "three nights of the month of Samhain," *trinouxtes Samoni*, in Gaulish, and *trenae Shamhna* in Old Irish. Variations of modern Celtic calendars show that Latin month names replaced some native month names and that there was local variation of month names in pre-Christian times. The evidence also shows that certain month names were widespread in the elder Celtic calendars, such as the "dark month" *Dumannios, An Dúdlachd, Mis Du,* or *Miz Du* which occured around the time of December to January on the Roman (Julian-Gregorian) calendar. But there were no months of Beth, Luis, Fern, Saille, etc., as misunderstood or invented by Graves. Furthermore, the real Celtic months were divided into fortnights beginning near the time of the first quarter of the new moon, with the second fortnight being either 15 or 14 nights, depending on whether the month was *matus*, "good, lucky" (30 nights long); or *anmatus*, "unlucky" (29 nights long). The older Celtic calendars were calculated by the Druids and show much in common with pre-Christian Greek, Teutonic, and Hindu calendars.

FESTIVALS

The year was called a *bleidoni* (12 months, or 13 in a leap year) and it was divided into two main seasons: *samon*, "summer,"and *giamon*, "winter." A *sonnocingos*, "solar-march," was the term for a solar year of 365.5 days. A year (or bleidoni) had four festivals: Samhain (Sah-win), Oimelc (Im-elg), Bealtaine (Byel-tin-uh) and Lughnasadh (Loo-nuh-suh). There were no celebrations of solstices and equinoxes, as many modern-day neopagans have erroneously assumed. Such festivals as Yule, Ostara, Saturnalia, Mid-summer, Charming of the Plough, Lupercalia, and Walpurgisnacht are alien to the Celts. The Celts knew nothing of these festivals in pre-Christian times, and yet the church borrowed many pagan festivals from many cultures. Candlemas, Lammas, and Hallowe'en are Celtic festivals that were Christianized; May Day became a spring festival.

Offerings were probably made at every full moon, or around the sixth night of a month when the moon was waxing. This night was called the *iuos* (ee-wawss) and the second fortnight was called the *atenouxtes*, "re-nights" or "again-nights," when the moon was waning. Daily prayers to the sun were probably made at dawn, like the Teutonic greeting of Sunna or the Hindu-Brahmanic Gayatri. Most Celtic festivals actually began on the 15th night of a month. Lughnasadh actually lasted for a whole fortnight (two weeks), or sometimes longer! It was a sort of Celtic version of the Olympic games, but held annually.

ESCHATOLOGY

Eschatology is the end of time in a religious system. Celtic eschatology is not "linear," but cyclical like the Hindu and Teutonic cycles of time. The Teutons believed in *Ragnorok*, which would mark the ending of this age when the world would be destroyed by fire and ice, then the gods and giants would fight it out and the world would be reborn in a new creation. Hinduism teaches of *kalpa*, in which a new beginning would come after the destruction of the cosmos. Similar beliefs were taught by the ancient Druids in which fire and water would destroy the manifested world. Strabo spoke of such doctrines being preached by Gaulish Druids. Such prophecies are found in the Norse *Voluspá*. These ideas are Indo-European in origin and are probably the source of doctrines of the ressurection of humanity on the Day of Doom in Christianity. To the Celts, though, death was the ending of the manifested body and integrated form; the entrance of the transcendent spirit to the upperworld and non-transcendent shadow to the underworld. Your own living soul went to your descendants, or descendants of your relatives, to be reborn. The shadow is the ghost or *púca* (spook) and *taibhse* which may haunt places. This is the Celtic explanation of poltergeists and hauntings. The shadow might take on a bodily shape. It is taking control of the *púca* (shadow) and *anatios/anatia* (spirit) that we call self-transformational magic; the highest form of magic, the magic of self-discipline.

Celtic Magic

The Druids and Filídh were known for their divination and mysticism (both of these are forms of magic, for certainly magic is not limited to spells of grimoires of the Hermetic tradition). These things took many forms, such as learning verse forms for composing blessings and curses, or memorizing the elder hymns, chants or incantations. The basic song was called a *cantalon* in Gaulish or *cetal* in Old and Middle Irish. Another verse form was called a *lay* or *laedha* in Old Irish. Thus, certain forms of poetry or verse were used for accomplishing effects. Words, singing and poetic speech were considered magical in Celtic culture. A Druidic spell is thus accomplished by singing a certain kind of song. References to these songs have even been found in ancient Gaulish inscriptions, as well as the Filídhecht school curricula. A lot of this lore is found preserved in Irish texts such as the *Book of Ballymote,* and formed part of the fifteen year training in the Filídhecht or "Bardic" schools.

Irish Filídh also had to learn *ogams* which were numerals, ciphers and codes made from notches carved along the straight edge of a twig. Ogams were primarily primitive numerals and mnemonic devices, but they were later used for memorizing and spelling out the sounds of the early Irish language and for divination. There were originally 20 ogam characters, but in mediaeval times the Filidh invented an extra five, called *aicme forfeda,* "group of extra woods (letters)," for consonant clusters or diphthongs. Lists of trees, animals, hills, bodies of water and so forth were all part of the ogamic system. It was the names of the trees that became associated with the ogam alphabet. Nowhere in the old Irish authorities does one find any evidence for the ogams representing months, nor did they represent lines from the *Song of Amergin* or the *Cad Goddeu*, "Battle of the Trees." Although there were ogams representing trees, trees themselves represented many things, such as playing pieces in board games like Irish *fidhchell,* "woodskill" (Welsh *gwyddbwyll*), or *brandubh,* "black-raven." Trees could also represent people, since people were descended from the world-tree *Bilios* (*Bile* in Irish).

14

Irish poet-magicians such as the Filídh graduated from the Bardic schools with the highest degree as an *ollamh* (oll-uv), a mediaeval Irish version of a master's degree or PhD. The *ollamh ré filídhecht* was granted many privileges that only high Druids held in pre-Christian times. They were expected to work as masters of ceremony for all royal occasions and to be advisers to their kings. They were certain other specialists such as the Brehons who specialized in law, and there were *seanchaídhe* or *shanachies* who specialized in history, stories, and genealogy, as well as singers (Bards), musicians, physicians, and healers who went through similar training.

Ceremonies such as the *tarbhfeis* (tarrvaysh), "bull-dream," involved a type of incubational divination; similarly the *imbas forosnaí* (imviss fo-ros-nee) was an incubation or lucid dream state induced with an incantation and splashing of animal blood or water on the cheeks. Many of these incubations involve sleeping or dreaming on the hide of a sacrificial bull or ox. Many magical techniques of the Filídh are found not only in the *Book Of Ballymote* or *Book of the Dun Cow*, but also in Cormac's *Glossary* and in the Fenian tales.

The *adbertos* (ahd-bayr-tawss) (Welsh *aberth*, Old Irish *idhbairt*) was the basic ceremony or offering. It is the sacrifice or communion with the Gods similar to the Hindu *yajna* or Norse *blòt*. One of the most famous ones is the *Epomeduos* which was carried out in mediaeval Ireland according to Giraldus the Welshman. It involved the marriage of a chieftain or king to a mare. The mare was immolated, then eaten by all who attended this ceremony. It has survived in the form of hobby-horse dances in modern folk custom. The most simple form of an adbertos is to simply bless a portion of food and offer it on a fire, or bury it in sacred ground. The usual traditional food used in modern-day Druidiactos is oatcakes and mead or beer, but other foods may be used. Such ceremonies are done at all festivals and gatherings, and they have many functions or purposes.

In modern Western magical thinking, such a ceremony as an adbertos could be considered a form of magic, just as the rites associated with Cabalistic grimoires are collectively referred to as ceremonial magick. But in the Celtic system, there is no need for using the Hermetic system of blending astrological hours, certain stones, colors, the Cabalistic sefirot, banishing rituals, circles, pentagrams or the like, since they are foreign practices and can be discordant or confusing when incorporated in the Druidic system.

There are many groups which try to blend the Celtic system with non-Celtic systems such as Cabala, Wicca, American Indian, Voodoo, Teutonic and Greco-Roman, but such a blend probably does no justice to any of these systems. A particular religious system should be studied deeply and practiced within its own cultural context. Many tribal and folk religions were never meant to be synchretized with other folk religions and universalistic religions. Such systems as Christianity and Buddhism often will absorb and synchretize local beliefs and customs, as long as this does not interfere with its main doctrines. Allowing an ancient ethnic folk religion to be revived is like keeping an endangered species alive, or preserving a minority language and/or culture. Mixing it up with other religious traditions may rob it of its full strength and dilute it to mediocrity. The key to true universal understanding is understanding a religious system in its own context and tolerating others' different beliefs rather than forcing them to fit your own.

DRUIDIC VESTMENTS

The appearance of the Druid is known to us from two main sources: Greco-Roman writings and Mediaeval Irish tradition. There is also evidence from Irish and Scottish folklore. Druids wore white tunics which in early Ireland were knee-length. The concept of them wearing full white robes is formed from the misunderstanding of the English translations of Pliny who mentioned *candida vesta*, "white garments," in reference to gathering mistletoe. He did not say white robes, but white garment or white clothing. He was probably describing a tunic and perhaps a cloak also. This also formed a part of the clothing worn in Highland Scottish inaugurations of clan chiefs, as worn by the chief bard. Both Irish and Scots tradition mention the rod or scepter of straight white wood gilded with metal, and this has been confirmed by archaeology. The rod or scepter was carried as a badge of office.

Irish tradition also speaks of cloaks of bird-feathers of the Filídh, cloaks of grey or white bull-hide of the Druids, and Bards wearing plaited or braided hair. Druids were often described as bald (such as the many Druids with the nickname *Mael* — Old Irish for "bald"). The bald head was probably a Druidic tonsure, presumably the same kind of partially shaved head used by later Irish clerics and condemned by the Roman church as non-conformist. This kind of tonsure is made by shaving the front of the hair from the top, ear to ear, all the way forward to the hairline. This gives the appearance of a receding hairline or of a very high forehead. It is interesting to note that Indian Brahmans have a very similar tonsure! One Druid named Mogh Ruith was described as wearing a speckled bird headdress; perhaps a sort of bird hat or helmet which had fluttering wings. It is true that Druids used gilded bronze sickles for cutting

16

sacred herbs for healing (e.g., Pliny's report of the mistletoe gathering) but there is no tradition of them carrying the sickles around as an emblem of their office.

There is no mention of Druids going either bearded, mustachioed or clean-shaven. It was a typical Gaulish fashion in ancient times for men to sport a mustache. Gallo-Roman men appear in sculptural portraits with mustaches and long sideburns, which were considered barbaric by Roman tastes. Celts preferred longer hair to the Roman styles; eventually the Roman fashion prevailed in Gaul for a few centuries, until Germanic fashions came into style after the invasion of Burgundians, Franks and Goths.

Celtic women dressed in ankle-length frocks with pleats, or pleated ankle-length skirts with tunics. Often an attractive white apron was tied to the shoulders and covered the entire frock or tunic and skirt. A cloak or tartan shawl was the Celtic fashion from ancient times to the present day. The traditional red skirt was worn by women in the Gaeltachts. One description of Druids fighting the Romans at Anglesey mentions priestesses wearing black; this is presumably because they are cursing the enemy, or it could be a representational image of the war-goddess Catubodua or Badb Catha, the "war-crow." The cloak or shawl of the bendrui or ueleda is drawn over the head when practicing ceremonies or offerings. Celtic women wore plaited or braided hair in many different styles, in pigtails or rings and buns.

Both Celtic men and women wore shoes of rough hide and the *breccan,* or tartan, wool fabrics. The tartan or breccan style was worn all over the Celtic world, though today it is associated chiefly with Scotland.

All Celtic nobility wore the *maniacis* (mah-nyah-kiss), or collar, which was often an open front neckring made of tubing or twisted silver, bronze or gold. The maniacis collar, or "torque," is associated with belonging to one's touta or *sliocht* (tribe or sept). The ancient *tricoros* symbol, or "triskele," has been found on an ancient pre-Christian *bracteate* (medallion) in Ireland. The tricoros is an ancient solar symbol representing the divine presence of *Nemos,* or heaven, the abode of the high Gods.

THE DRUID'S GEM

Pliny the Elder, in his *Natural History,* mentions the Druids manufacturing an object called the *ovum anguinum,* or "snake's egg," which in Gaulish would be called *ouion natracos.* This is known in British and Irish tradition as the snake's gem, or Druid's gem. The

Druid's gem was a round bead about 1 to 1½ inches or so in diameter, decorated with spirals or swirls. It was sometimes made out of ceramic (as in Scotland), glass (reported in Wales, Scotland, Cornwall) or, as sometimes in ancient Gaul, out of empty whelk egg cases or despined sea urchin shells. According to Pliny, a Gaulishman who was a Roman citizen wore an *ovum anguinum* to court for good luck, but lost his case because the Roman magistrate was prejudiced against him for wearing a Celtic charm.

The snake which dwells in the underworld is said to have been the origin of these charms. Mythically, snakes in the underworld are always guardians of sacred treasures such as the salmon in Irish tradition, Fafnir in the Volsunga Saga, and snake in the garden of Eden. Snakes as guardians of mysteries and treasures of the underworld is a theme which goes back to a source common to both Indo-Europeans and Semites.

NEMETON: SACRED SPACE

A clearing marked off for ritual was called a *nemeton* in Gaulish. The shape of the nemeton was either square or rectangular, or sometimes round. The square or rectangle represents the heavens. Round nemetons represent the earth and the manifested realm, and were used for royal inaugurations. The ancient nemeton of Emhain Macha (Ardmacha) was unearthed at Navan Fort in Armagh. The trunk in the center showed signs of animal blood offered on it. Scholars have speculated that this may have well been the famous *Craebh Ruadh*, "Red Branch," that was used in reference to the Ulster heroes under King Conchobhar Mac Nessa. This Red Branch was the emblem of Ulster, of the Ulaid (Uoluntioi) during this time of ancient Ireland.

NEO-DRUIDISM SINCE THE 1700s

The last vestiges of the Filídhecht schools were destroyed in the 1600s when the Elizabethan English conquered and murdered the last of the Gaelic culture of Ireland. The "plantations" of Ulster and the extension of the Pale beyond Leinster into Munster and all the way to Connacht wiped out the old Gaelic aristocracy and their culture. Cromwell came later, and sent off many Irish leaders to "Hell or Connaught!"

In Scotland, a few Bards and Vates were left in the Gaelic areas of the Hebridean islands, but the old Gaelic order was in for more

English oppression. Ironically, it was the English who first took an interest in the Druids of antiquity in the 1700s. William Stukeley fancied that they were the builders of Stonehenge and other "henges," or megalithic monuments. Naively, the English Masons invented mock orders of Druidism incorporating various speculative ideas with flights of fancy. Welshmen such as Edward Davies took off with these new fads during the Age of Enlightenment when Romanticism was growing as a movement against the Age of Reason. The pendulum swung, and when the Romantic era began Edward Williams dubbed himself "Iolo Morganwg" and invented his own form of Druidism, or "Bardism," and forged documents which he attributed to a Welshman named Llywellyn Sion.

He wrote his forgeries in Welsh and had them published with his own English translations as the *Iolo Mss* by the Welsh Manuscript Society in the early 1800s. Later, a volume of more of his forgeries were published posthumously as the *Barddas*. The *Barddas* (1862) was edited by John Williams ab-Ithel in two volumes. It was proudly hailed as a book of ancient Welsh mysticism, but unfortunately it was judged a fraud as early as the late 19th century. In the 20th century, it was proven to have been a forgery by G. J. Griffiths. Iolo Morganwg was trying to establish a great bardic tradition for South Wales to compete with North Wales, but in so doing he faked an historical basis of Druidism surviving into the 1600s. He claimed that the information he presented came from these earlier bards such as Llywellyn Sion. While he helped to establish a southern Welsh *eisteddfod* (eye-stedh-vod) tradition, he created a phoney Neo-Druidism which reflects Deism, Unitarianism and Neoplatonic ideas. His doctrines of reincarnation with a place of punishment in Annwn, a place called "Abred" for this world, Gwynfyd for heaven, and "Ceugant" for God reflects Platonic and Aristotelian metaphysics, as well as Deism. He invented the *coelbren y Beirdd*, which is a primitive version of the modern Welsh alphabet of Latin letters designed for carving in wood. He invented the motto *Y Gwir yn erbyn Y Byd*, "The truth against the world," and four "Albans," Hefin, Elfed, etc. The three vertical lines called a *trilithon*, or rays of Awen or inspiration, are also his creation. Other concepts include the *dasgubell rhod*, the Hirlas horn, the Gorsedd and the mistranliteration of Uates as "Ovates." He must have been well-read in the classical commentaries, but he knew nothing of Irish tradition which better preserved Druidic tradition. The Gorsedd of Bards, "Ovates," and Druids at Welsh *eisteddfodau* and the organizations which spawned English Druidic Orders (such as the ones that were run by

Thomas Maughan and Ross Nichols) had incorporated the pseudo-Druidry of Morganwg (Williams) into their degree workings. Later, ideas from Gardnerian Wicca were incorporated, as well as the usual Hermeticism and Cabalistic grimoire magic, or ceremonial magick. Sadly and ironically, it seems that Neo-Druidry made up for its lacking in authentic Druidism by borrowing materials from various other systems. But then Druidism is Celtic religion, and therefore one would expect to find Celtic religion better represented in a Celtic country such as Ireland or Scotland than in England, but unfortunately Wales has been more dominated by English culture than Ireland.

Celtic culture blossomed in Ireland's literary Renaissance of the late nineteenth century. In Ireland, even Anglo-Irish writers such as W. B. Yeats, Douglas Hyde and others became enthralled with Ireland's Celtic past. Renewed interest in folklore and folk custom set the scholars, philologists, folklorists, and musicians off collecting materials in Ireland's *Gaeltachts* (Gayl-tokhts), where people still spoke Irish Gaelic as an everyday language.

This was when the great mediaeval Irish books were getting translated and published. Great scholars such as George Calder, Robin Flowers, Lady Gregory, R. A. Stewart Macalister, Rudolf Thurneysen, Osborn Bergin, Myles Dillon, T. F. O'Rahilly, and Sean Delargy made great contributions to the study of Irish historical and literary antiquity. Great ancient Celtic stories were finally being translated and influencing Ireland's modern day bards and poets.

Similarly in Scotland, a great Celtic renaissance spread to the Highlands. Indeed, interest in early Celtic folklore began in Scotland after the James MacPherson forgeries were exposed. MacPherson had claimed to have collected ancient Celtic lays from the Fenian cycle. But it was MacPherson himself who had composed them in the original Gaelic, though he claimed he had discovered them. In his Fenian tales, Finn mac Cumhail was called Fingal, and Oisín (Usheen) was called Ossian (Awshin). MacPherson's Fenian material was so influential that the Romantic movement's passion for mediaeval literature spread because of the popularity of his literary creations. Even symphonic music was composed under the inspiration of MacPherson's Fingal and Ossian stories, and it was very popular on the continent.

In the latter half of the nineteenth century, Alexander Carmichael began collecting Highland material from folklore. It was still published long after his death, but his eight volume collection *Carmina Gadelica* is a great source of late forms of Celtic folk magic.

In modern America, the Druidic movement had a hazy beginning with North American versions of the Druid Orders of England. Later, in the twentieth century, interest in Irish romanticism grew during the time of Irish emigration, but Irish- and Scottish-Americans' Celtic interest was limited, and unfortunately many Welsh-Americans forgot their Welsh roots, since their ancestors came over in the 1700s.

From London, the late Colin Murray ran an organization called the G.S.O. (Golden Section Order) and published beautifully hand-colored illuminated newsletters called the *New Celtic Review*. In Scotland, the Keltic Research Society was formed by J. A. Johnston, "Kaledon Naddair," who published the *Inner Keltia* journal, reprints of folktales, and *The Pictish Shaman*. He set up a College of Druidism in the early 1980s out of "Caer Aedin," or Edinburgh, teaching Cabalah and Iolo Morganwg's Barddas tradition, as well as some genuine Celtic lore. Celtic religion seems to be the main interest of only a few groups today, for most of them are focused on Mother Goddess worship or Pan-European mixed with Neopagan Wicca. There are several "groves" and other covens of Dianic Wicca, most of which are devoted to Mother Goddess worship and to Robert Graves' *The White Goddess*. Except for a few scattered Celtic groups around the English-speaking world, Druidiactos, headquartered in America, is one of the few purely Celtic spiritual and cultural movements. It has spread from Australia to Quebec and France. Druidiactos is not just another neopagan organization, it is a Post-Modern Celtic Renaissance movement starting on the grass roots level. The Breton Druids' organization (allied with Druidiactos) is called Comardiia Druuidiacta Aremorica. They publish materials in French which authentically represent a revival of the Druidic or Celtic religious system. Their *Ver-Druis* (Chief Druid) is called *Esunertos,* and their *Allio-Ver-Druis* (Assistant Chief Druid) is *Gobannogenos*.

I lead the Druidiactos organization and *Uxsello-Druidiaxton* (Druidic college). I am known to my Breton colleagues by their translation of my first name into Gaulish: *Tasgos* (Gaulish for Tadhg). The *Allio-Ver-Druis* is *Uindoderuos* (M. G. Boutet) of Quebec. The Celtic spiritual path is Druidism, which is the magic of the *Druídecht* (modern Irish *draíocht*) of the Druids, the Filídhecht (Modern Irish *filíocht*) of the Filídh, and the Celtic magic of the whole Celtic culture and mythology.

Not everybody is a "Druid" in the Celtic path of Druidiactos anymore than all Hindus are Brahmans, or all Christians are priests, bishops, or ministers, or all Jews are Rabbis. The Druid is the priest of the people of the Celtic path. His or her job is to direct the ceremonies, to make sure no mistakes are made in the ritual, to organize the gatherings and to help others. The Celtic path also has the Warriors, the martial arts traditions, chivalry, manners, and etiquette.

Druidiactos is also very much a cultural organization devoted to studying the Celtic ways, past and present, to preserve the ancient Celtic heritage for today and for the future generations. Many of these Celtic ways are being preserved in the *Gaeltachts* of Ireland and Scotland, in many areas of Wales, Brittany, and Cornwall, but it is also found in North America in Nova Scotia, in the Appalachian mountains, and in many large cities around the United States and Canada. There are Celts in Australia and New Zealand who preserve their heritage in these nations, as well.

Druidism is not the Bardism of Iolo Morganwg, not the British-Israelite faith, not Cabalism, not Neo-Platonism, not Pythagoreanism, not Wicca, nor is it Feminist Mother Goddess worship. It is the cultural and spiritual heritage of the Celtic peoples, a polytheistic religion derived from the archaic proto-Indo-European past. It was carried into Western Europe by those Indo-European folk who spoke the Celtic dialects.

The Celtic folk, with kings, druids, warriors, farmers and herdsmen, settled and conquered Western Europe and taught those stone-age peoples to use bronze, to speak Celtic, and of the magic of Druidism.

THE FUTURE OF DRUIDISM

As long as there are people who remember their Celtic heritage and its contributions to modern culture and civilization, and the legends, folk-tales, and myths of the Celtic peoples, there will be those who dream about the ancient Celtic magic, the heroes Finn, CúChullain and all of the other heroes, deities and places. I wrote *The Sacred Cauldron* for such people and in order to bring a deeper understanding and appreciation of the Celtic system.

Where one finds the Irish Celts one finds those whose roots may go back to the elder Druids and other learned men of old Ireland: Druids (O'Droody, Drury < Ó Druada "descendent of the Druid"), the Filidh (Neeley, McNeely, McNeilly < mac an Fhiledh "son of the fili"), healers (Hickey, O'Hickey < Ó h-Iceaidh "son of the healer"), or bards (Ward, MacAnward < Mac an Bháird "son of the bard"), the satirist (MacCrossan, McEncrossin, McCrossen, Crossen, Cross, Crosbie, Crosby < Mac an Chrosáin "son of the satirist"), the smith

(O'Gowan, McGowan, Gowan, McGahen < O Gabhain/ O Gobhain "descendent of the smith" and Mac Gobhain "son of the smith"), and the Brehon or judge (Abraham, O'Brahan, <O Breithemháin). The Old Irish learned class became known as the *Aes Dána* or "men of arts," and this title became hereditary during the mediaeval period. That is how names were passed on, as well as professions, and after the English conquests many Gaelic names were Anglicized by translation or by re-spelling them to resemble English names and words, or to simplify the pronunciation. Welsh and Scottish names went through similar Anglicizations.

We are entering the Post-Modern era; people are returning to their roots both spiritually and culturally. Resources are scarce; the earth and its atmosphere cannot stand any more pollution; we must end the population explosion. Technology may have led to many of our problems of over-production, but it will also lead to solutions to our problems. We must allow ourselves and others to grow spiritually and individually while using these new tools for the better of humankind instead of the destruction of our natural resources. People are not going to be able to afford materialistic and greedy lifestyles in the near future. Spiritual paths such as Druidism will mean more to us because they emphasize family, hearth, and home; a natural lifestyle in harmony with the ecology of the cosmos, and the diversity of peoples and their ethnic cultures. People will find pleasure in fine books, folk music, and in simple fellowship with friends and family. There will be less time and money to spend gossiping over the decadent life styles of the rich and famous. More people will be turning their energies toward productive ways of cleaning the environment and avoiding the waste of precious resources.

Druidism is a spiritual path that is in harmony with the natural flow of the cosmos. It is one of the many folk religions, or "earth" religions, that brings people back into reverence for living things. It brings people back into the discipline of hard work and productivity, physical strength and health, and following the wisdom of one's ancestors as opposed to throwing out the ancient wisdom of past generations and "reinventing the wheel." In tribal or folk religions, the elders are respected for their experience and the insight they have gained from their age. This is how it will be in the Post-Modern era. The old modernist view dictated that everything must be changed and that the older generation had been all wrong. In the Post-Modern era, tough times may come and go, but people will return to what has always been true and what has always worked in the past, what works in the present and will work in the future. The return of the American-Indian peoples to their native traditions, the Japanese to Shinto, African Americans to African traditions, the Germanic peoples to Asatru or Troth, Indians (Hindus) to Sanatana Dharma, and Celts to Druidiactos are religions of the Post-Modern era.

This trend is anti-racist and anti-ethnocentrist because it allows people to be what they are and to grow within their own cultural identity and not to be forced into a universal and ecumencial monolith of one religion for all humankind. Universalism and synchretism forces all people to conform to one way.

Some new-agers and neo-pagans would like to unify all religious systems under one monolithic and synchretistic system in the pursuit of cultural relativism, but such a system actually implies that the smaller ethnic religions are somehow inferior and should be subsumed into one large religious empire. Would it not be better to allow many diverse systems, pure and true to their own traditional systems, than insisting that they blend with other incompatible practices and beliefs? True religious tolerance must go beyond synchretism and superficial unity.

The "new age" isn't really new at all; instead, it is a time for many old ideas to be revived. We will see the return of the Celtic religion of Druidiactos, "Druidism," with its high gods, the Tuatha Dé Danann or *Aes Sídhe*, "folk of peace," or *Daoine Sídhe*, "people of peace," and the local land and water goddesses, with the priesthood of *Druides*, "druids;" *Uates*, "prophets;" *Gutuatres*, "invoking priests;" and *Bardoi*, "bards."

Nemetons will be re-built similar to the ancient ones on sacred, unspoiled land consecrated to the powers of the cosmos. People will feel more kinship to the local natural environment and weather patterns as they will have less need to travel in fuel-burning engines as they interface in the virtual reality of their computer systems.

It is up to future generations to seriously research the ancient ways of their ancestral faiths, and reconstruct the the wisdom of the past so that it will live in the present. This means going back to the original sources and asking the elder Druids from native traditions using critically sound and scientitifc methods of reconstruction instead of re-inventing Druidism from the fancies and fictions of the modern redactors, revisionists, and poseurs.

GLOSSARY

adbertos (Gaulish) — an offering or ritual in which something is given to the Deuoi.

Andumnos (Gaulish) — the Underworld/Otherworld or Nether-world which corresponds to the Greek Elysian Fields and Tartaros or the Teutonic Valhall and Hel. There are many isles of the Celtic Otherworld. Andumnos was later called *Annwn* in Welsh, *Andomhain* in Early Irish (Gaelic).

ategenos (ah-teh-gen-awss) — "rebirth;" an incarnation or manifes-tation of a trait, talent, concept, spirit, or divinity into human form. It is usually something genetically passed down.

bardos, plural *bardoi* (Gaulish, Brittonic, Goidelic) — this is the old Celtic term for a singer or minstrel who sang praises of great heroes and chieftains, or sang satires (curses and insults).

brehon (from Irish *breithamháin*) — this was the mediaeval Irish judge or jurist; a specialist of the old Druidic class that survived Christianization.

Celt (pronounced *Kelt*) — the name of the ethnic group ancestral to the Irish, Scottish, Welsh, Cornish (of Cornwall), Breton, Manx, and a high percentage of the French, Belgian, and Swiss peoples. *Celtic* (Keltic or Seltic) and *Celtophile* (keltofile or seltofile) are derivatives of this word. People who belong to the Druidiactos movement are called the *Keltoi* (kel-toy); singular *Keltos* and *Kelta*.

CúChullain (Koo-Khullin) — the great epic hero of the old Ulster stories such as the "Cattle Raid of Cooley;" called the *Táin Bó Cuail-nge* (Toyn Bo Koo-ling). He was the incarnation or manifestation of the Celtic high God of Lugus (Lugh or Lleu).

Druid — the English word derived from the Latinized word for a Celtic priest and teacher who was a judge, lawyer and prime-minis-ter of the ancient Celtic kingdoms and tribes. In old Celtic, this word was *Dru-wis, Druis* in Gaulish, *Druí* in Old Irish, *Dryw* in Old Welsh. In modern day Celtic religion, a Druis or "Druid" is the minister of the Celtic religion, much like a Purohit or Pundit in Hinduism, a Pastor or Rector in Christianity, a Rabbi in Judaism, an Elder in the Troth, a Mobad in Parseeism. In most Non-Celtic "Druidisms" today, the term "Druid" is given to all practioners as if all were members of a clergy or priesthood. This is mostly the practice of the misinformed borrowing and capitalizing on the name of the venerable Celtic priesthood.

Druidiactos (also **Druidiaxtos**) — the name of the Celtic religious movement which is a return to the traditional pre-Christian values, customs and faith of the Celtic peoples. The name is a reconstructed form of the Old common Celtic word for "druidism," just as Brahmanism is sometimes used synonymously for the Vedic religion of ancient India.

filí (fee-lyeh) — a poet-magician, or "seer," who performed Celtic magic and mystical rites. The Filí was a solitary practitioner, something like a shaman in other cultures.

Finn Mac Cumhail (Finn Mok Kool) — the great hero and incarnation (manifestation) of Uindos, "Cernunnos," son of Noudons in a group of great epic tales and romances called the Fenian cycle.

geis or **geas** (gayss), plural *geassa* (gassa) — a controlling spell or enchantment in which a certain action or behavior will cause another certain action or effect. Usually it takes the form of a taboo or a destiny as when CúChullain overheard Cathbad say that any boy who accepts weapons on that day will be destined to be a great hero, and he asks his king for arms.

lebor (l'yower) — Old Irish word for book.

Noudons (Noh-dawns) — Celtic God who represents the old retired king, a wizard and mystical grandfatherly figure. He is the blemished king, wild old man God and law-giver. He is called *Nuada Airgetlamh* (Noo-uh Arriget-louw) in Old Irish, *Nudd* (Neethe) or *Lludd Llaw Ereint* (Hleethe Hlouw Air-eint) in Welsh.

ogam (oh-um) — the notches and lines carved on sticks and stones by the Irish Filídh and other learned folk.

P-Celtic — the Gaulish-Brittonic language from which Cornish, Breton and Welsh descend.

Q-Celtic — the Goidelic or Ancient Gaelic language from which Old Irish evolved and developed into Middle Irish, then modern Irish, Gaelic (Scots Gaelic) and Manx Gaelic. Irish calls four and five *ceathair* and *cuig* (ka-her and koo-eeg), Scots Gaelic calls them *ceithair* and *coig* (keh-her and koyk).

sidhe (shee) — "peace" in Old Irish, thus *Aes Sidhe*, "people of peace," is a name for the spirits and ghosts of the Otherworld.

touta (toh-oo-tah, toh-tah) — a tribe or kindred of people who come together regularly. A local community. In Druidiactos, a congregation of people who regularly meet on a monthly basis, or at least four times a year to celebrate Celtic festivals.

UerDruis (also **Verdruis**) — the leader of the Celtic religious movement. This is simply the word Druis with the prefix *Ver*, "over," and therefore a Verdruis is literally the supervisor or superintendent of the Druidiactos movement and organization. In ancient times, a Ver-Druis was simply the Druid who hosted the gathering of the toutas in one of the great ritual centers such as Carnutes (Chartres), later Lugudunon (Lyon) in Gaul, or Teahmhair (Tara) in ancient Ireland.

BIBLIOGRAPHY

Carmichael, Alexander, *Carmina Gadelica*. Edinburgh: Oliver and Boyd, 1900.

Carey, John, "Listening to the Celts" in *Gnosis*, Fall 1988.

Cross, Tom P., and Clark Harris Slover (editors), *Ancient Irish Tales*. Chicago and N.Y.: Barnes and Noble, 1966.

Davidson, Hilda Rogerick Ellis, *Myths and Symbols in Pagan Europe*. Syracuse: Syracuse University Press, 1988.

Delaney, Frank, *The Celts*. Boston: Little and Brown, 1986.

DeVries, Jan, *Keltische Religion*. Stuttgart: Kohlhammer, 1961.

Dillon, Myles, *Celts and Aryans: Survivals of Indo-European Speech and Society*. Calcutta: Indian Institute of Advanced Study, 1975.

Godwin, David, *Light in Extension*. St Paul: Llewellyn, 1992.

Herlihy, David, *Mediaeval Households*. Cambridge, Massachusetts: Harvard University Press, 1985.

Kelly, Aidan, *Crafting the Art of Magic*, Volume One. St. Paul: Llewellyn, 1991.

Littleton, C. Scott, *The New Comparative Mythology*. Los Angeles: University of California Press, 1982.

Lincoln, Bruce, *Myth, Cosmos and Society*. Cambridge, Massachusetts: Harvard University Press, 1985.

MacCrossan, Tadhg, *The Sacred Cauldron*. St. Paul: Llewellyn, 1991.

_____ , *The Way of the Druid: a Handbook of Real Celtic Magic*. Forthcoming.

Matthews, Caitlin, *Elements of the Celtic Tradition*. Wellingborough: Element Books, 1989.

Piggott, Stuart, *The Druids*. London: Thames and Hudson, 1968.

Polome, Edgar C., "Some Thoughts on the Methodology of Comparative Religion, With Special Focus on Indo-European" in *Essays in Memory of Karl Kerenyi*, Journal of Indo-European Studies Monograph Series Number 4. Washington: Institute for the Study of Man, 1984.

Rees, Alwyn and Brinley Rees, *Celtic Heritage*. London: Thames and Hudson, 1961.

Rose, Elliot, *A Razor for a Goat*. Toronto: University of Toronto Press, 1989.

Thorsson, Edred, *A Book of Troth*. St. Paul: Llewellyn, 1989.

_____ , *The Truth about Teutonic Magick*. St. Paul: Llewellyn, 1990.

Webb, James, *The Occult Underground*. LaSalle, Illinois: Open Court Press, 1974.

STAY IN TOUCH

On the following pages you will find listed, with their current prices, some of the books now available on related subjects. Your book dealer stocks most of these and will stock new titles in the Llewellyn series as they become available. We urge your patronage.

To obtain our full catalog, to keep informed about new titles as they are released and to benefit from informative articles and helpful news, you are invited to write for our bimonthly news magazine/catalog, *Llewellyn's New Worlds of Mind and Spirit*. A sample copy is free, and it will continue coming to you at no cost as long as you are an active mail customer. Or you may subscribe for just $7.00 in U.S.A. and Canada ($20.00 overseas, first class mail). Many bookstores also have *New Worlds* available to their customers. Ask for it.

Stay in touch! In *New Worlds'* pages you will find news and features about new books, tapes and services, announcements of meetings and seminars, articles helpful to our readers, news of authors, products and services, special money-making opportunities, and much more.

TO ORDER BOOKS AND TAPES

If your book dealer does not have the books described on the following pages readily available, you may order them direct from the publisher by sending full price in U.S. funds, plus $3.00 for postage and handling for orders *under* $10.00; $4.00 for orders *over* $10.00. There are no postage and handling charges for orders over $50.00. Postage and handling rates are subject to change. UPS Delivery: We ship UPS whenever possible. Delivery guaranteed. Provide your street address as UPS does not deliver to P.O. Boxes. UPS to Canada requires a $50.00 minimum order. Allow 4-6 weeks for delivery. Orders outside the U.S.A. and Canada: Airmail—add retail price of book; add $5.00 for each non-book item (tapes, etc.); add $1.00 per item for surface mail.

LLEWELLYN PUBLICATIONS
P.O. Box 64383-577, St. Paul, MN 55164-0383, U.S.A.

THE SACRED CAULDRON
by Tadhg MacCrossan

Here is a comprehensive course in the history and development of Celtic religious lore, the secrets taught by the Druids, and a guide to the modern performance of the rites and ceremonies, as practiced by members of the "Druidactos," a spiritual organization devoted to the revival of this ancient way of life.

The Sacred Cauldron evolved out of MacCrossan's extensive research in comparative mythology and Indo-European linguistics, etymology and archaeology. He has gone beyond the stereotypical image of standing stones and white-robed priests to piece together the truth about Druidism.

The reader will find detailed interpretations of the words, phrases and titles that are indigenous to this ancient religion. Here also are step-by-step instructions for ceremonial rites for modern-day practice.
087542-103-2, 304 pgs., soft-cover, illus.   **$10.95**

CELTIC MAGIC
by D. J. Conway

Many people, not all of Irish descent, have a great interest in the ancient Celts and the Celtic pantheon, and *Celtic Magic* is the map they need for exploring this ancient and fascinating magical culture.

Celtic Magic is for the reader who is either a beginner or intermediate in the field of magic, providing an extensive "how-to" of practical spell-working. There are many books on the market dealing with the Celts and their beliefs, but none guide the reader to a practical application of magical knowledge for use in everyday life. There is also an in-depth discussion of Celtic deities and the Celtic way of life and worship, so that an intermediate practitioner can expand upon the spellwork to build a series of magical rituals.

Presented in an easy-to-understand format, *Celtic Magic* is for anyone searching for new spells that can be worked immediately, without elaborate or rare materials, and with minimal time and preparation.
0-87542-136-9, 240 pgs., mass market, illus.   **$3.95**